SPRINGS & FLUSHES

SCOTLAND'S LIVING LANDSCAPES

Acknowledgements: Ben Averis, Sandy and Brian Coppins for information on lichens;
Des Thompson, Dave Horsfield, Derek Ratcliffe and John Baxter for comments

Author: Alison Averis

Series Editor: John Baxter (SNH)

Design and production: SNH Design and Publications

Photography:

A. Averis cover right, 7 bottom right, 13 top right; **L. Campbell** cover top middle,19, 25 left, 25 right, 26 top left, 26 top right, 26 bottom left, 26 bottom right, 28, 29 top, 29 bottom; **L. Gill/SNH** cover bottom left, frontspiece, contents, opposite foreword, 1, 2, 3 top, 7 left, 7 top right, 9, 13 top left, 13 bottom right, 14, 15, 17 top left, 17 bottom, 18 top, 18 bottom right, 20, 21, 22 top, 22 bottom left, 22 bottom right, 23, 32 bottom left, 32 right, 35, 36, 38 bottom, 40, 41, 43; **G. Logan** 4, 11; **B. Meatyard/University of Warwick** 34 right, 38 top; **J. Petrie/Inverness Museum and Art Gallery** 31; **D. Ratcliffe** opposite introduction, 3 bottom, 8, 16, 18 bottom left, 32 top left, 34 centre; **B. Renevey/SNH** 27; **D. Thompson** 42; **M. Usher** 13 bottom left, 17 top right, 34 left; **D. Whittaker** cover top left.

Illustrations:
Clare Hewitt 5, 6 & 37.

Scottish Natural Heritage
Design and Publications
Battleby
Redgorton
Perth PH1 3EW
Tel: 01738 444177
Fax: 01738 827411
E-mail: pubs@snh.gov.uk
Web site: http://www.snh.org.uk

Cover photographs (clockwise from top left):

1. Four spotted chaser dragonfly
2. Adder
3. Hillside spring dominated by the bright green moss *Dicranella palustris,* among rushes and *Nardus* grassland
4. Flush, Ariundle National Nature Reserve

SPRINGS & FLUSHES

SCOTLAND'S LIVING LANDSCAPES

by

Alison Averis

Contents

Boggy flush with sedges and *Sphagnum* mosses

High in the Cairngorms, streams and flushes flow from melting snow and tiny springs

Foreword

Springs and flushes are not the most obvious components of the Scottish landscape unless you accidentally step into one and get wet feet! These habitats generally occupy small areas in the Scottish uplands and as a result are often missed or ignored by naturalists. Because these are specialised and localised habitats, they support a fascinating and diverse flora and fauna, including several nationally rare plant species. They provide important micro-habitats for many animals, flowering plants, mosses and liverworts.

In this booklet Alison Averis presents a lively and wide-ranging account of Scottish springs and flushes, one of the truly neglected habitat types in Scotland. Besides introducing us to where springs and flushes occur, and their plant and animal life, she explores the role of springs in Scottish culture and the vexed question of what might be in bottled Scottish mountain spring water. She also discusses the ever-increasing problems of conservation in relation to land-use, pollution, and climate change.

Alison has considerable practical experience of Scottish upland vegetation and ecology based on many years of devoted fieldwork in Scotland. She uses her wide-ranging field knowledge and keen eye for habitats and plants to provide an excellent, enjoyable, extremely readable, and thorough introduction to Scottish springs and flushes. She elegantly and eloquently shows that despite their small extent, springs and flushes are an important, integral and fascinating part of Scotland's Living Landscapes; they are full of biological and cultural interest.

H. John B. Birks

Professor H. John B. Birks
University of Bergen & University College, London.

Snow bed hollows with springs and flushes on the plateau of Aonach Beag, near Ben Alder

Introduction

The hidden jewels of the hills

Imagine a walk in the hills. Picture a landscape of dark sweeping moorlands rising to wide horizons, or of stony slopes carved by ice into dramatic corries and soaring summits. Think of the scents of grass and heather and peat, and of the sweet spicy bog myrtle. Bring to mind the peace and stillness. And then notice what initially sounds like silence to the urban ear, accustomed to the constant noise of traffic, voices, television, radio and machinery. Slowly the silence resolves itself into the natural sounds of the hills and uplands: the wind ruffling the vegetation, the songs of skylarks, the evocative calls of grouse, curlew and golden plover.....and more often than not the sound of running water.

Now look more closely at the vegetation: the patchwork colours of the bogs, heaths and grasslands; ochre-gold and green, purple and brown. See that here and there they are stitched with long green lines of rushes or sprinkled with jewel-bright patches of mosses and liverworts. Among these you might see glints of water appearing as cascading sequins. These are springs and flushes.

Bog mosses including the red-coloured *Sphagnum capillifolium*

Their place in the landscape

A purple mat of the liverwort *Scapania undulata* dotted with the green starry shoots of the moss *Polytrichum commune*

What are springs and flushes?

'Spring' and 'flush' are terms used to describe the vegetation or assemblages of plants on wet irrigated ground.

In simple terms, a spring is the source of a stream: the point where the water bubbles or flows out of the ground. The actual upwelling of water is usually covered with a cushion of mosses, and the rill or streamlet emerges at the downslope edge of the patch of mosses. Flushes on the other hand mark out places where water flows over of the ground more diffusely. Flushes vary from expanses of soil, gravel and stones with a sparse array of mosses, sedges, rushes and small flowering plants to dense green swards of sedges or rushes or both interleaved with small herbs and underlaid with a carpet of mosses and liverworts. Where water emerges over a large area of ground it is common to see colourful patchworks or mosaics of springs and flushes: the mossy spring-head vegetation occurring around the upwellings of water and the more drab flush vegetation covering the ground where the flow of water is slower and more diffuse.

Coire Ardair, Creag Meagaidh: rich in springs and flushes

Montane spring with mosses and liverworts

Where do springs and flushes occur, and why?

Springs and flushes occur throughout the upland parts of Scotland. Though we think of them as elements of the vegetation of open ground, they also occur in woodland under the shade of trees. They are especially associated with hills and moorlands because of the wet upland climate. In general, there is more rain, snow and mist in upland regions than there is in the lowlands. The rain, mist and melted snow soak into the ground, saturating the soil and keeping the water-table high, or close to the surface of the ground. The water-table is all important; it is the upper limit of permanently saturated ground, below which water fills all the spaces in the rocks. Springs and flushes occur where the water-table reaches the surface of the ground. Flushes also often occur where the soils are saturated with water which is seeping slowly downhill through the soil rather than in a distinct channel as a rill or stream.

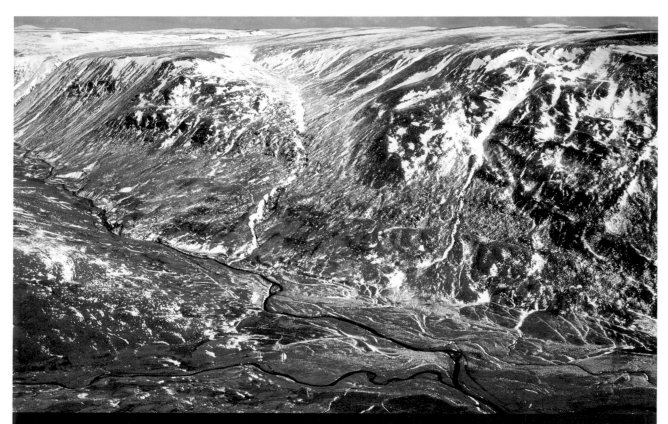

River Isla: an area rich in montane springs and flushes

The source of rivers

It is always exciting to follow rivers and streams right to the source. The flow of water gradually diminishes from a wide stream up to a tiny trickle, and it is impossible to know in advance whether you will arrive at a place where water gushes out vigorously from a brilliant green, red and orange cushion of mosses and liverworts or at a place where water seeps out through peat and mud from a tall green patch of rushes.

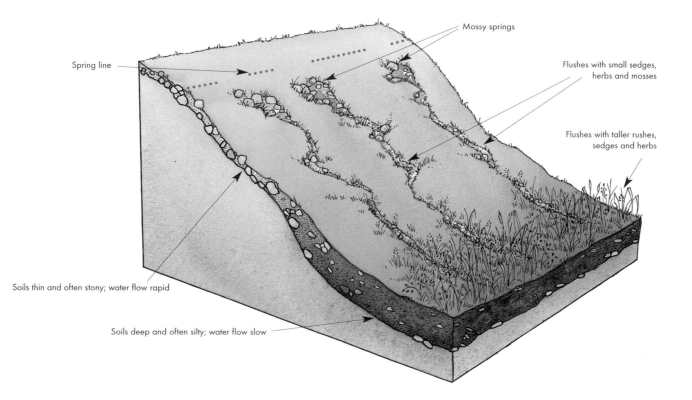

Spring line

Mossy springs

Flushes with small sedges, herbs and mosses

Flushes with taller rushes, sedges and herbs

Soils thin and often stony; water flow rapid

Soils deep and often silty; water flow slow

Typical pattern of springs and flushes in relation to topography and soils

The environment of springs and flushes

As in all habitats, the plant and animal life of springs and flushes is largely determined by the physical environment. Here the qualities of the irrigating water are especially important.

The water may gush out strongly, producing a copious stream within a few metres of the source, or it may seep out slowly. In general, the slower the flow of the water, the more likely it is that a wide range of plants will be able to become established.

The water temperature in any particular spring or flush is usually fairly constant, but it can vary between pleasantly cool and bitterly cold. The coldest springs, on the shaded slopes of the highest hills, are home to a few specialised mosses and liverworts which are able to grow when the temperature is very low - often around 4°C: the temperature of the average domestic refrigerator!

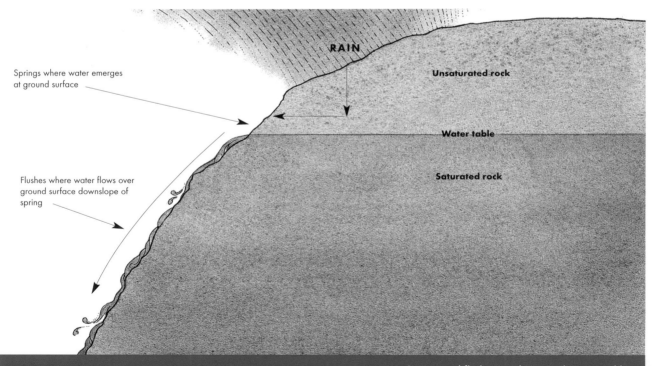

RAIN

Unsaturated rock

Water table

Saturated rock

Springs where water emerges at ground surface

Flushes where water flows over ground surface downslope of spring

Springs and flushes in relation to the water-table

Moss-dominated spring

Flushes are common among West Highland bogs and heaths

Stony mountain habitat with golden-coloured moss
Palustriella commutata, and bog mosses: Kinloch Hills, Skye

The mineral content of the water is determined by the chemical composition of the rocks from which it emerges. As water flows through the ground before emerging as a spring or flush, it becomes charged with mineral salts dissolved out of the rocks and soils. The composition of this load of dissolved salts determines which plants will grow in the places where the water emerges. Where the rocks are alkaline or rich in lime and other plant nutrients, the plants which grow in the springs and flushes are very different from those that are able to grow where the water is acid and deficient in lime. Indeed the water of some springs and flushes is so highly-charged with lime that it is precipitated out in the form of calcium carbonate, forming a grey-white, porous, crunchy crust over the surface of the ground. This stony crust is known as tufa, from the Latin word *tofus* meaning 'a soft stone'.

The surface of the ground where the water emerges is also important. The plant and animal life in different springs and flushes can vary dramatically as a result. Some springs and flushes have a base or substratum of bare rock or stones, and the array of plants in these is usually open and sparse. In some springs and flushes there is a thin layer of soft, saturated mud. In others the plants may be growing on a base of peat. The springs and flushes on wet muds tend to be the most densely-vegetated and to have a rich fauna of invertebrates, but those on peat are often very acid and inhospitable, and sustain few plants or animals.

Dr Dave Horsfield (SNH) surveying flush vegetation

Most strongly lime-rich springs and flushes

The distribution of springs and flushes

The widest diversity of springs and flushes is to be found on the plateaux and in the high corries of the central and eastern Highlands, where these wetland communities in anastomosing networks spread bright sheets of colour over the grey stony landscape. Lime-rich springs and flushes are most common in the Breadalbane Hills, which run across the southern part of the Highlands from Ben Lui in the south-west to the hills around Caenlochan Glen in the east. There are also many lime-rich springs on the Moorfoot, Lammermuir and Tweedsmuir Hills in the Southern Uplands.

Highest montane springs and flushes

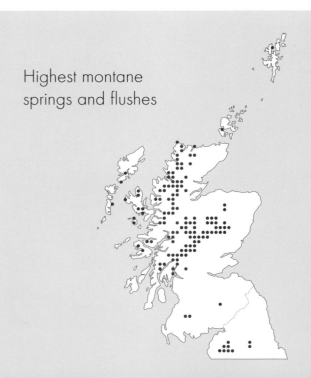

Carn an Tuirc: many streams and burns originate from springs high up in montane country

Plant life in springs and flushes

Which plants grow in springs and flushes, and why?

The most common and often the most noticeable plants in springs and flushes - because of their bright colours - are the mosses and liverworts, collectively known as bryophytes. Many sedges and rushes, a few grasses and a number of small flowering plants are at home in these wet places too. A few specialised lichens live in springs and flushes.

Bryophytes and lichens have no roots. Although mosses and liverworts are fixed to the ground by thread-like filaments, called rhizoids, most are unable to draw up water and nutrients from the soil or water in the way that most other plants do. Instead, they absorb water and nutrients directly through their leaves and stems from water flowing over and around them, and from the moist atmosphere. The lichens which grow in springs and flushes form a thin crust over rocks and pebbles, anchored to the stone by a network of fungal threads or hyphae which grow tightly around the mineral crystals which make up the rock. These plants, like the bryophytes, absorb water and nutrients from the water which flows over them.

Unlike the flowering plants, bryophytes and lichens have no waterproof outer skin or cuticle to stop them losing moisture to the atmosphere, and can dry out very quickly in dry weather. This is why many of them are so much at home in springs and flushes, where there is an almost constant supply of fresh aerated water which is enriched with nutrients from its passage through the earth. Even the most vigorous springs can fail when the water-table drops in an exceptionally dry summer, and there are times too when the water is locked up as ice. When times are hard, bryophytes and lichens survive by not growing. They stop photosynthesising and wait in a state of suspended animation for the return of favourable conditions. Different species of mosses, liverworts and lichens vary in the time they can endure without water, but even the most sensitive species are able to survive for a few days.

Life is totally different for the so-called 'higher plants': the shrubs, sedges and grasses and small flowering herbs which have a root system, and so obtain their water and nutrients from the soil. Though there are usually ample supplies of plant nutrients in springs and flushes, only a few higher plants can tolerate perpetually waterlogged conditions as their roots cannot develop properly where there is too little oxygen in the soil. Plants which can grow in very wet places generally have a system of air-spaces between the cells in their roots. In the centre of a spring, the mat of mosses and liverworts often closes over the upwelling of water, forming a thin skin of vegetation over the water. The small herbs and grasses which grow among the bryophytes here have their roots in water rather than in soil: a natural example of the 'hydroponic culture' used to grow strawberries and vegetables such as cucumbers and tomatoes.

Heath spotted orchid, common in upland flushes

Moss-dominated spring

Dwarf cudweed, characteristic of snow-melt flushed ground

Oblong-leaved sundew, found in western flushes and bogs

Stream flowing over *Jungermannia exsertifolia* (liverwort) with *Philonotis fontana* (moss) in foreground

Plants in springs

The most characteristic species of the lime-rich springs is the moss *Palustriella commutata*, which grows in swelling green and orange cushions scattered with grasses and often a few small herbs.

Where the water is acid the most common plant is the bright green moss *Philonotis fontana*. Its distinctive erect shoots form dense cushions which are often dotted with starry saxifrage, or with the opposite-leaved golden-saxifrage. Another common moss of acid springs is *Dicranella palustris*, which has short spiky shoots of an almost fluorescent brilliant yellow-green. The bog moss *Sphagnum denticulatum*, with its stout curved red-gold shoots, is a common plant in springs which emerge through peaty soils. The most common liverwort in springs is *Scapania undulata*, which has glossy flattened shoots in varying shades of red, brown and purple. The most characteristic lichen in acid springs is *Polyblastia cruenta*, forming an inconspicuous dark brownish-green layer over submerged stones. *Hymenelia lacustris*, which is a distinctive bright orange colour, is often also common on stones in springs.

Moss-dominated spring on mountain plateau

Plants in flushes

In the open, stony and lime-rich flushes you may see plants such as butterwort with its pale green greasy rosettes of sticky leaves, and yellow mountain saxifrage: a plant with fat grey-green leaves and, in summer, tumbling cascades of starry golden flowers. Flushes at higher altitudes are home to the uncommon three-flowered rush with its spiky green leaves and oval brown flowers. Sedges grow in flushes too and you will usually find the grey-green tufts of carnation sedge and also the yellow sedge, which as its name suggests has leaves of a rich yellow-green. These lime-rich flushes can have a strong sulphurous smell of decomposing vegetation.

Taller and more continuously vegetated flushes occur wherever the lie of the land concentrates the flow of surface water into hollows, gullies and the level bottoms of glens. The most common plants here are the sedges and rushes; grass-like plants with narrow leaves and small, brownish or greenish flowers. The sedges most often encountered are common sedge and star sedge. Bottle sedge forms distinctive tall, grey-green swards, often around the shores of lochs. Flushes consisting of soft rush or sharp-flowered rush fill gullies and hollows running down the hillsides and spread out in vast mires on the lower slopes and in the glens.

Superficially, these tall flushes may all look much the same. But the bryophytes which clothe the ground and the flowering herbs which twine among the rushes and sedges vary a great deal according to whether the water which irrigates the flush is acid or lime-rich. In the acid flushes the ground is covered with a green layer of *Sphagnum* mosses and there are few flowering herbs. In some peaty acid flushes plants such as cross-leaved heath, deer grass, and bog asphodel with its spires of orange-gold flowers in late summer can be found. The peaty soils in these flushes have a sparse covering of mosses such as the bog-moss *Sphagnum capillifolium* and the dark green-black *Campylopus atrovirens*. The insectivorous sundews often dot the dark carpets of mosses. In the lime-rich flushes the *Sphagnum* mosses are usually replaced by other mosses such as *Calliergonella cuspidata*, a large plant with conspicuous red stems and long, pointed green shoots. They may also have a rich array of flowering plants such as meadowsweet, angelica and water avens.

Yellow mountain saxifrage

Butterwort, a common plant of flushes

Three-flowered rush, a scarce plant of base-enriched mountain flushes

Bog mosses *Sphagnum capillifolium* (red) and *Sphagnum papillosum* (ochre) in an acidic, boggy flush

Marsh marigolds, Unst

Marsh St John's wort

Northern marsh orchid

Coastal springs and flushes

Springs and flushes near the coast, particularly on the west coast, experience a mild and equable climate and can accommodate warmth-loving species which are generally more common further south in Britain. Marsh St John's wort can sometimes be found in wet flushes near the sea in the south-west Highlands and the Hebrides. It is an attractive creeping plant, holding its bright golden flowers above a mat of round silvery hairy leaves which sparkle and glisten with tiny drops of water. Another inhabitant of these flushes is the bog pimpernel, with tiny round leaves borne in pairs and delicate bell-shaped pale-pink flowers.

Dunlin

Springs and flushes of the highest hills

Many of our most spectacular and beautiful springs and flushes occur in cold sheltered hollows and corries on the high hills where snow lies all winter and far into spring. Distinctive assemblages of plants known as snow-bed communities occupy the hollows and gullies where the snow lingers longest. There are some sheltered slopes on the higher hills in the Highlands where snow-patches persist for most of the summer. Here the vegetation may be exposed for only a few weeks each year. Bryophytes and a few lichens are almost the only plants which can grow in such places. These plants are able to photosynthesise under snow where there is too little light for other plants to survive. Many bryophytes also contain anti-fungal chemicals so that they do not go mouldy in the still, cold, humid atmosphere. In these snow-beds there can be great spreads of the moss *Pohlia wahlenbergii* var. *glacialis* with its translucent apple-green leaves and red stems. When it grows in a patch around a spring the effect can be stunning, with the waxy-textured leaves beaded with innumerable drops of water. (The Latin epithet *glacialis* means 'icy' and is a reference to the temperature of the water where this moss grows, as well as to its snowy habitat.)

Grey-green mats and patches of the tiny liverwort *Anthelia julacea* are characteristic of channels and gullies where melt-water runs from a thawing snow-patch. Its dense mats are often studded with tiny flowering plants such as dwarf cudweed and the dwarf alpine form of marsh marigold. These springs are often set in the pale blond swards of mat-grass which mark out places where snow lingers into spring.

The flushed soils which are irrigated by the water from melting snow in the late spring and early summer, and by the water from cold high-altitude springs, may be clothed with swards of sedges. These include the russet sedge with its distinctive heads of black flowers, and the white sedge which has small cream-coloured flowers.

Part of a mountain spring (foreground) on Ben Hee, Sutherland

Hillside with streams, springs and flushes

Primroses on the damp banks of a woodland stream

Opposite-leaved golden saxifrage

Meadowsweet

Springs and flushes in woodland

Most of the moorlands and lower hillsides in Scotland were once covered with trees, and springs and flushes would have played a natural part in this woodland vegetation. Nowadays, we are so used to seeing springs and flushes on grassy or heathery slopes that it seems quite odd to come across them under trees. Yet they are just as common here as they are on the open hillsides. They look just like their counterparts on the open slopes and there is an equally wide range of communities: small mossy springs; tall rush-mires; short, open swards of sedges and small herbs. The moss *Palustriella commutata* forms dense golden-green cushions around spring-heads in woodland on lime-rich soils, and in more acid woods mosses such as *Sphagnum denticulatum*, *Dicranella palustris* and *Bryum pseudotriquetrum* are all able to grow in the moderate shade cast by a canopy of trees. Flushes occur in damp glades and along the banks of woodland streams. Swathes of sedges and rushes winding in wet ribbons down the hillsides under the trees are often dotted with the bright flowers of buttercups, ragged robin, meadowsweet and marsh thistle.

Toad in *Polytrichum* moss in wet woodland

Life other than plants

Invertebrates

> *'Mosses are useful to the insect tribe,*
> *countless numbers of which find homes*
> *among their branches, and roam about in*
> *their shades as in mighty forests'*
> Frances Tripp, British Mosses, 1888

The spongy carpets of mosses and liverworts in springs and flushes seem like a thin skin of vegetation to us, but to tiny invertebrates they are a vast forest providing shelter and food. Many organisms live in the aerated and often nutrient-rich water, in the sloppy unconsolidated soils or among the crowded leaves of the bryophytes themselves. Most invertebrates have an annual life-cycle and are unable to survive in any particular place unless there are suitable conditions for breeding every single year. Springs and flushes are especially valuable habitats for invertebrates because they are permanent elements in the landscape. The flow of water may be slow, but it usually flows throughout the year. The temperature and acidity (or pH) of the water are also fairly constant.

Anyone looking at mosses and liverworts through a microscope will also see tiny animals moving among the leafy shoots. These microscopic aquatic animals can occur in unimaginable numbers. It has been calculated that a square metre of *Sphagnum* moss can be home to 16 million protozoans (simple single-celled or colonial animals).

Among the invertebrates which are visble to the naked eye, the flies (Diptera) are the organisms most often associated with bryophytes in springs and flushes. The crane flies (Tipulids) are some of the most conspicuous. They live in and feed on mosses. In summer the adults emerge in huge numbers when the empty pupal cases are obvious, sticking up out of the bryophyte carpets like tiny chimneys.

Spiders are really common too, especially the fast-moving wolf spiders which are easy to see as they run over the cushions of mosses and liverworts in search of prey.

Worms live in the soil in springs and flushes. Water-beetles and their larvae lurk among bryophytes, looking out for prey. Their prey may include aphids and mites, some of which feed on the bryophytes themselves.

In the vicinity of springs and flushes on warm summer days, dragonflies and the smaller damselflies dart hither and thither. These large insects are often spectacularly coloured in shades of gold, fiery red and metallic blue and green.

Damselfly on bog asphodel

Black darter dragonflies on ling

Red grouse

Northern wheatear

Dotterel

Common snipe

Birds

The Scottish hills are rightly famous for the red grouse, a bird which occurs nowhere in the world outside Britain and Ireland. The chicks of red grouse, and its montane cousin the ptarmigan, feed upon invertebrates, and the supplies of these in springs and flushes are crucial for successful breeding. Other upland birds eat invertebrate food throughout their lives. The most conspicuous of these are the upland waders: curlew, golden plover, dotterel, dunlin, greenshank and snipe. But our hills are also home to small insect-eating birds such as wheatear, ring ouzel, skylark, meadow pipit and the elusive and rare snow bunting. All of these depend to a greater or lesser extent on the great abundance of insect food in the springs and flushes. Snipe and woodcock often remain in the hills over winter when the springs and flushes are especially important. They usually remain liquid, because of the moving water, when the rest of the ground is frozen hard, and are a vital refuge where birds can come to feed.

For birds which breed in the uplands it is important that feeding and breeding habitats are sufficiently close together. This has been shown clearly for the dotterel: a fascinating and colourful upland wading bird. It has been discovered that dotterels need a combination of moss heath for nesting, and springs, flushes and snow-bed grasslands as a source of insect food for their young. The young leave the nest almost as soon as they are hatched and need to feed on insects within hours.

The swards of rushes on the lower ground and around the upland fringes are important nesting and feeding sites for lapwing, redshank, snipe and curlew.

Lapwing

Other animals

The insects, spiders and other invertebrates are the food supply for many upland animals and birds. Frogs abound in upland springs and flushes, and toads and viviparous lizards hunt here too. Frogs and lizards are food for adders, which may be observed basking on a warm cushion of *Sphagnum* or on a tussock of grass.

Sheep, deer and goats graze in springs and flushes. Indeed their trampling and poaching may help to maintain springs and flushes by keeping the cover of vegetation open and preventing the encroachment of trees and shrubs. However, in some places deer can badly damage springs. They wallow in springs and flushes in summer, coating themselves with peat in order to discourage flies and to protect themselves from the heat of the sun. Intriguingly, sheep seem to come to the flushes to die: their corpses are often found in wet rushy places. Perhaps they get entrapped in these wet, marshy areas, or perhaps some other purpose brings them there to die.

Red deer stag about to wallow in a deep flush

Common lizard

Adder

Springs, flushes and people

Springs, culture and customs

> *'Tha cluanaig ann an iomall sléibh*
> *far an ith féidh lus biolaire*
> *'na taobh sùil uisge mhór réidh*
> *fuaran leugach cuimir ann'*
>
> *(At the far edge of the mountain there is a green nook*
> *where the deer eat water-cress,*
> *in its side a great unruffled eye of water,*
> *a shapely jewel-like spring)*
> *From Sorley Maclean 'Fuaran', 1943*

Springs, wells and water have long been an important part of human culture. 'Fuaran' or 'fhuarain', the Gaelic for 'a spring', appears in many hill names. A good example is Beinn an Fhuarain in Assynt, where a long south-facing slope is striped with the vivid green lines of mossy springs. Water must always have been a preoccupation with people in Scotland, given our wet climate. Water has been associated with sanctity from earliest times and is or has been used in the rituals of many religions. In prehistoric times wells, springs and rivers were often associated with pagan goddesses, and in Christian times with saints. Tobermory on the island of Mull is Tobar Moire or Mary's well. The well can still be seen in an old ruined chapel close to the town. Tibbermore just to the west of Perth is also

Mary's well or perhaps big well Tobar Mór. Wells and springs dedicated to St Mary or St Bride were frequently fertility sites, resorted to by young women on the eve of marriage in the hope of guaranteeing that children would be born. Holy wells were often regarded as places of healing, with certain wells associated with particular afflictions. The 'cloutie wells' are a survival of this belief. Sufferers hung strips of cloth from trees beside the well, and as the cloth decayed so did the affliction disappear. A number of wells and springs became the site of religious pilgrimages and were regularly visited over many years.

Rituals associated with wells and springs persisted into the 20th century. For example there is a well-known cloutie well on Culloden Muir. In 1937, a crowd of over 12,000 people assembled here to drop coins in the water, drink from the well, wish for something and tie a rag to one of the nearby trees. Still today, you pass areas such as these with rags tied to trees near wells!

The cloutie well at Munlochy, Black Isle

A Highland spring with *Pohlia ludwigii* (moss) and *Nardus* snowbeds

The Glenlivet Distillery

Lagavulin Distillery

Mountain springs and bottled spring water

The relationship between mountain springs and the liquid sold in bottles as mountain spring water is not always as straightforward as the labels on the bottles would have you believe. For a start there is no such thing as a Scottish mountain spring with naturally fizzy water, so anything you buy with bubbles in it has had carbon dioxide added in a processing plant.

According to European and British legislation, 'natural spring water' must come from an unpolluted underground source, must be free from microbial contamination and must have received no treatment apart from filtration to remove sand and silt. Water sold as 'spring water' usually comes from an underground source but does not have to be bottled on the spot. It may be treated to alter its chemical composition or to remove pathogenic organisms. Nevertheless of 29 brands of still bottled waters sampled by 'Which' in April 1991, almost all were contaminated by large numbers of bacteria. It is worth noting that adding a slice of lemon to a glass of spring water does more than improve the taste: the citric acid in the lemon juice is also a potent killer of many bacteria!

Water may be extracted from springs either from a natural exit or from a bore-hole. Where the water emerges in a natural spring at the surface of the ground, the source is enclosed by a box or tank to shield the supply from pollution. The water flows into this collecting tank and is piped out to be filtered and then either bottled or transported for further processing. This, of course, means that the plant life of the original spring does not survive.

City-dwellers accustomed to paying high prices for bottled water may envy the inhabitants of the more isolated parts of Scotland, where untreated natural spring water comes out of the taps and people bathe and wash their clothes in it as well as drinking it. Many people have a private supply, drawing their own water from their own spring. It is usually necessary to construct a tank or chamber around the spring to collect the water and build up a head of pressure so that the water can be piped to the house.

Scottish spring water is the basic liquid from which whisky is made. It imparts a finer taste to tea than treated tap water, and, of course, makes wonderful porridge!

In many ways we all depend on springs and flushes. Fill a glass with water and some of the molecules in that water may well have bubbled out of a tiny mossy spring high in the hills. The water from springs and flushes fills our reservoirs and is piped to houses, factories, shops, offices and hospitals, and drives turbines to generate electricity.

Conservation and land-use

Why are springs and flushes important?

These habitats form some of the most natural parts of the landscape. They are the product of landform and geology; of the fundamental structure of the land. So although they are small they may have existed essentially unchanged for thousands of years, while the surrounding vegetation may have changed beyond all recognition. At high altitudes, springs are among the last remnants of late-glacial terrestrial vegetation left in Britain. Snow-bed springs and flushes would have been common throughout Britain as the ice from the Pleistocene glaciations began to retreat about 10,000 years ago. Many Scottish springs and flushes look exactly the same as those in the hills of Norway, where there is not nearly so much grazing as there is in Scotland and where the vegetation owes more to variation in the natural environment than to the changes wrought by people. The Scottish Highlands are the most important part of Great Britain for the springs and flushes of snow-beds and many types are not found south of the Highland Line.

From the upland margins, including upland woods, to the tops of the highest hills, each spring or flush is unique, containing a fascinating variety of tiny plants. Though water flow, temperature and chemistry and the texture of the ground play the main parts in determining what plants grow in which springs or flushes, much of the variation is also the result of the chance establishment of one species rather than another.

Here too, there are many of our rare mountain plants. One beautiful rarity is the starwort mouse-ear chickweed, a plant of cold acid springs at high altitudes. Less spectacular but equally rare and valuable are brown bog-rush, once thought to be extinct, and false sedge. Both grow in lime-rich flushes in the central Highlands. On the hills around Moffat, there are interesting lime-rich flushes with uncommon plants such as the creeping forget-me-not. The rare Iceland purslane grows only in a few stony flushes on the basalt hills of Skye and Mull.

Creeping forget-me-not   Starwort mouse-ear chickweed   Iceland purslane

The trickle from a spring high in the mountains can lead to cascading waterfalls

How are springs and flushes affected by land management?

Springs and flushes are especially valuable as oases of natural vegetation within more managed landscapes where heaths have been burned and woodlands cleared. The springs and flushes on the lower hill slopes might be rather different in an ungrazed landscape. Occasionally you may come across a big spring which has been fenced off to stop sheep and cattle wandering in and drowning. If the spring is fairly low down - below about 400m - you may find that the carpet of bryophytes has been lost under a tall sward of grasses and robust herbs such as sorrel and meadow buttercup.

In the absence of grazing many springs and especially flushes might look very different, with the bryophytes, sedges, rushes and herbs hidden under low bushes of willow. The flushes with a tall sward of rushes or bottle sedge almost all represent the ground-layer vegetation of wet woodland which has been able to persist without a canopy of trees.

Draining wet hillsides, whether by ploughing for forestry or by cutting moor-grips, can do much damage to the natural patterns of flushes.

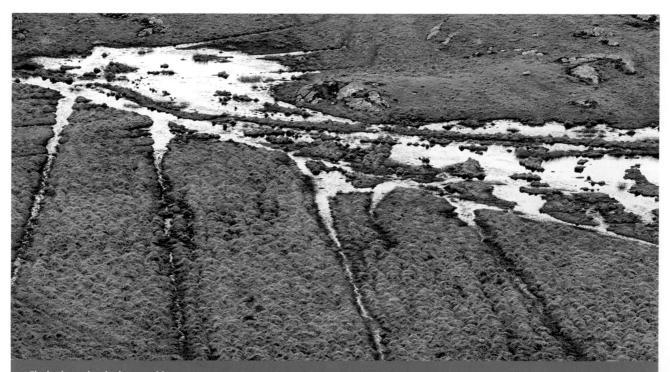

Flushed peatlands damaged by moor-grips

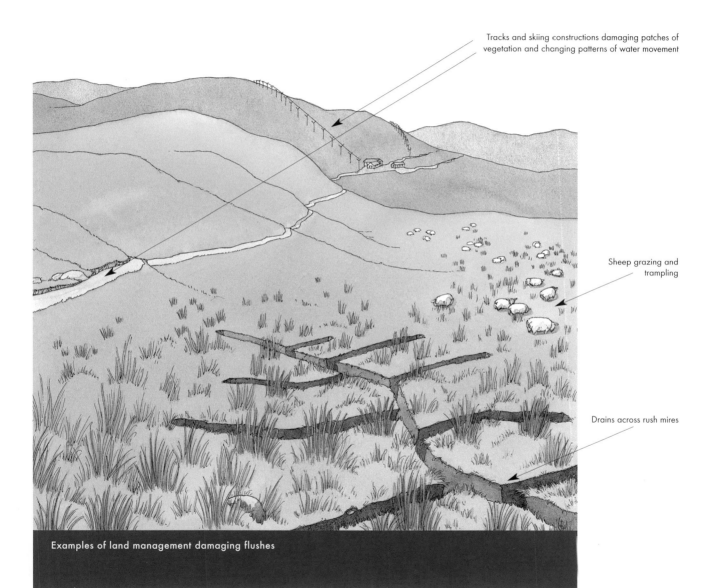

Tracks and skiing constructions damaging patches of vegetation and changing patterns of water movement

Sheep grazing and trampling

Drains across rush mires

Examples of land management damaging flushes

Iceland purslane research, Mull

Red deer can cause considerable damage by trampling

Pollution and a changing climate

Although pollutants may be filtered out of spring water during its passage through the ground, airborne pollution can damage the vegetation of springs and flushes. Plants may be killed outright, or their growth or reproductive processes may be hindered. Mosses, liverworts and lichens are especially susceptible to acid rain because they derive water and nutrients directly from their surroundings and from the atmosphere. Though the Scottish Highlands are far from the main sources of atmospheric pollutants, there is still a considerable fallout of nitrogen and sulphur from the combustion of fossil fuels (including vehicle emissions) and industrial processes. This is because of the heavy rainfall over the hills. Pollutants are often borne on easterly winds from eastern Europe as well as from more southern British cities. Mist as well as rain can deposit pollution on the vegetation, and the effect is greater when rain is actually falling through a cap of cloud.

A particular problem faced by the springs and flushes at high altitudes is that they may be covered by polluted snow. Snowflakes accumulate pollutants from the air as they fall, and sometimes the snow which covers the ground can actually be grey with soot. When the snow melts in spring it releases a sudden concentrated pulse of polluted water: the so-called acid flush which can prove fatal to many species and which has even been known to kill fish many miles downstream. The effect of this on the plants in the springs and flushes seems to depend on whether or not they are in active growth at the time they are inundated with polluted water. Plants which are actively growing in places where the snow has retreated are damaged more than those which are still protected by a covering of snow.

A changing climate might pose a serious threat to some of our springs and flushes. Many permanent springs and flushes might fail or become intermittent in a warmer or drier climate. If less of the annual precipitation falls as snow, and if the snow which falls does not persist so long, the characteristic vegetation of late snow-beds might be lost. The most likely casualty among the plants of snow-bed springs and flushes is the moss *Pohlia wahlenbergii* var. *glacialis*. This moss depends on a copious supply of cold water, much of which comes from melting snow. If there was not so much late-lying snow this species could lose ground to the more catholic *Philonotis fontana*, which can tolerate a wider range of conditions.

Man-made springs and flushes

Many of the species of springs and flushes are able to grow in drainage ditches and on wet disturbed ground. Patches of spring and flush vegetation can be seen on the irrigated gravel around disused mine workings and along the sides of roads and tracks in the hills. The abandoned lazy-beds around old crofting townships are often surprisingly good places to see flush vegetation. These relicts of former cultivation are easy to see, especially in the western Highlands and on the Outer and Inner Hebrides. They consist of parallel alternating strips of raised ground and hollows. Lazy-beds were designed so that water would drain out of the raised mounds down the channels either side. The raised strips would then be fertilised with cattle manure (and seaweed in coastal communities) and used to grow potatoes and cereals. Nowadays almost all have fallen into disuse, but flush vegetation has often developed in the drainage channels. Indeed channels among lazy-beds which are irrigated with acid water are among the best places to find the moss *Campylopus shawii*, a rare species of the Hebrides. It is a large and conspicuous plant, growing in a dense, golden-green turf of long shiny leaves.

High plateau flushes are important areas for insects and foraging birds

A last word

A necklace of green springs
On the golden slope of the Corrie
Among the sun-dazzled grasses the diamond glitter
And in the huge silence of the hills
The small cold voice
Of water among stones.

Autumn leaf fall stands out against the *Sphagnum* carpet

If you have enjoyed Springs and Flushes why not find out more about Scotland's distinctive habitats in our Scotland's Living Landscapes series. Each 'landscape' is a dynamic environment supporting a wealth of plants and animals, whose lives are woven inextricably together. The colourfully illustrated booklets explore these complex relationships simply and concisely, and explain why they are important and what needs to be done to protect them for the future.

Sea Lochs

Featuring dramatic underwater photography, this booklet tells why Scotland's sea lochs are so special to people living around their shores and to the magnificent wildlife that depends on their sheltered waters.
Sue Scott
ISBN 1 85397 246 0 pbk 24pp £3.00

Firths

Firths lie at the heart of Scottish life: they support our economy, house most of our population, and provide a precious home for wildlife. Discover the magic of our unsung firths and the efforts being made to secure their future.
Steve Atkins
ISBN 1 85397 271 1 pbk 36pp £3.50

Coasts

Scotland has nearly 12,000km of coastline, much of it remote, unspoilt and strikingly beautiful. Learn all about this changing environment, the unique habitats, landforms and wildlife and the many pressures they face.
George Lees & Kathy Duncan
ISBN 1 85397 003 4 pbk 28pp £3.00

Boglands

Bogland is one of Britain's most undervalued habitats. This booklet challenges the conventional view of boglands and rewards its reader with vivid images of the colourful and intriguing wildlife of bogs.
Richard Lindsay
ISBN 1 85397 120 2 pbk 20pp £3.95

Soils

As all gardeners know, what grows on the surface depends on what's beneath their feet. Indeed soils are home to a all sorts of animals as well as plants. This booklet relates the story of our soils to the landscapes we see everyday.
Andrew Taylor & Stephen Nortcliff
ISBN 1 85397 223 1 pbk 24pp £2.50

Kelp Forests

An essential introduction to this hidden kingdom. Discover the variety of plants and animals which live in the 'forests', find out why kelp forests are so important in Scottish waters and how healthy kelp forests help to prevent coastal erosion.
Ian Fuller
ISBN 1 85397 014X pbk 44pp £3.95

Grasslands

Grasslands form an important part of our natural heritage and this booklet looks at how they provide a vital habitat for birds, butterflies, animals and plants.
Stephen Ward & Jane MacKintosh
ISBN 1 85397 070 0 pbk 48pp £3.95

Mountains

Two thirds of Scotland is covered by mountains and wild uplands, which straddle geological and climatic boundaries to give us several distinct mountain areas. These special landscapes and their wildlife are vulnerable to intensive use and demand the highest standards of stewardship.
Mark Wrightham
ISBN 1 85397 326 2 pbk 40pp £4.95

SNH Publications Order Form:
Living Landscapes Series

Title	Price	Quantity
Sea Lochs	£3.00	
Firths	£3.50	
Machair	£3.00	
Coasts	£3.00	
Boglands	£3.95	
Soils	£2.50	
Kelp Forests	£3.95	
Grasslands	£3.95	
Mountains	£4.95	
Springs and Flushes	£4.95	

Postage and packaging: free of charge within the UK.

A standard charge of £2.95 will be applied to all orders from the EU.

Elsewhere a standard charge of £5.50 will apply.

Please complete in **BLOCK CAPITALS**

Name _____

Address _____

_____

_____
Post Code

Type of Credit Card VISA ☐   MasterCard ☐

Name of card holder _____

Card Number

☐☐☐☐ ☐☐☐☐ ☐☐☐☐ ☐☐☐☐

Expiry Date ☐☐ ☐☐

Send order and cheque made payable to Scottish Natural Heritage to:

Scottish Natural Heritage, Design and Publications, Battleby, Redgorton, Perth PH1 3EW

E-mail: pubs@snh.gov.uk   www.snh.org.uk

We may want to send you details of other SNH publications. Please tick the box below if you do not want this. We will not pass your details to anyone else.

I do not wish to receive information on SNH publications ☐

Please add my name to the mailing list for the   SNH Magazine ☐

Publications Catalogue ☐